Name:

Address:

Phone: Mobile/Cell:

Email:

Important Numbers:

Passport No: Driving Licence No:

Travel Insurance No: Camera Serial No:

Others:

Medical Information:

Blood Group: Doctor:

Allergies/Medication:

Emergency Contact:

Other:

Cover image: © Matt Munro

December 2016 / January 2017

MONDAY 26

Boxing Day
Day of Goodwill (South Africa)

TUESDAY 27

WEDNESDAY 28

THURSDAY 29

FRIDAY 30

Plan an Adventure

SATURDAY 31

New Year's Eve

SUNDAY 1

New Year's Day

Life is either a daring adventure or it is nothing. – Helen Keller

January 2017

MONDAY 2

TUESDAY 3

WEDNESDAY 4

THURSDAY 5

Start of Harbin Snow & Ice Festival (China)

FRIDAY 6

Epiphany

Plan an Adventure

SATURDAY 7

Orthodox Christmas Day

SUNDAY 8

Rivers know this: there is no hurry. We shall get there some day. – A.A.Milne

January 2017

MONDAY 9

TUESDAY 10

WEDNESDAY 11

THURSDAY 12

FRIDAY 13

Plan an Adventure

SATURDAY 14

SUNDAY 15

Not until we are lost do we begin to understand ourselves. – Henry David Thoreau

January 2017

MONDAY 16

Martin Luther King Day (USA)

TUESDAY 17

WEDNESDAY 18

THURSDAY 19

Start of Sundance Film Festival (UT – USA)

FRIDAY 20

Plan an Adventure

SATURDAY 21

SUNDAY 22

Travel is fatal to prejudice, bigotry, and narrow-mindedness. – Mark Twain

January 2017

MONDAY 23

Anniversary Day (Wellington – New Zealand)

TUESDAY 24

WEDNESDAY 25

Robert Burns Night (Scotland)

THURSDAY 26

Australia Day (Australia)

FRIDAY 27

Plan an Adventure

SATURDAY 28

Chinese New Year

SUNDAY 29

One's destination is never a place, but a new way of seeing things. – Henry Miller

January / February 2017

MONDAY 30

Anniversary Day (Auckland – New Zealand)

TUESDAY 31

Up Helly Aa Fire Festival (Shetland – Scotland)

WEDNESDAY 1

THURSDAY 2

Groundhog Day (USA)

FRIDAY 3

Plan an Adventure

SATURDAY 4

SUNDAY 5

Superbowl Sunday (USA)

I haven't been to everywhere but it's on my list. – Susan Sontag

Koggala, SRI LANKA

Koggala is home to a long, wide, stretch of beach. Here stilt fishermen perch precariously like storks above the waves at high tide. Each fisherman has a pole firmly embedded in the sea bottom, close to the shore, on which he perches and casts his lines. Highly coveted stilt positions are passed from father to son.

© Matt Munro

February 2017

MONDAY 6

Waitangi Day (New Zealand)

TUESDAY 7

WEDNESDAY 8

Culture Day (Slovenia)

THURSDAY 9

Start of Berlin Film Festival (Germany)

FRIDAY 10

Feast of St Paul's Shipwreck (Malta)

Plan an Adventure

SATURDAY 11

Tu Bishvat
Pingxi Lantern Festival (Taiwan)

SUNDAY 12

Two roads diverged in a wood and I – I took the one less traveled by, and that has made all the difference. – Robert Frost

February 2017

MONDAY 13

TUESDAY 14

St Valentine's Day

WEDNESDAY 15

THURSDAY 16

Independence Day (Lithuania)

FRIDAY 17

Plan an Adventure

SATURDAY 18

SUNDAY 19

Adventure is not outside man; it is within. – George Eliot

February 2017

MONDAY 20

Presidents' Day (USA)

TUESDAY 21

WEDNESDAY 22

THURSDAY 23

FRIDAY 24

Independence Day (Estonia)

Plan an Adventure

SATURDAY 25

SUNDAY 26

Carnaval Sunday (Rio de Janeiro – Brazil)

Travelling…it leaves you speechless, then turns you into a storyteller. – **Ibn Battuta**

February / March 2017

MONDAY 27

TUESDAY 28

Shrove Tuesday
Start of Carnevale (Venice – Italy)
Start of New Orleans Mardi Gras (LA – USA)

WEDNESDAY 1

Ash Wednesday
St David's Day (Wales)

THURSDAY 2

FRIDAY 3

Liberation Day (Bulgaria)

Plan an Adventure

SATURDAY 4

SUNDAY 5

*Don't tell me how educated you are, tell me
how much you travelled.* – Mohammed

March 2017

MONDAY 6

TUESDAY 7

WEDNESDAY 8

THURSDAY 9

FRIDAY 10

Start of South by Southwest Festival (TX – USA)

Plan an Adventure

SATURDAY 11

Independence Restoration Day (Lithuania)

SUNDAY 12

Purim
Start of Daylight Saving Time (Canada, USA)

There are only two emotions in a plane: boredom and terror. – Orson Welles

March 2017

MONDAY 13

Adelaide Cup (SA – Australia)
Canberra Day (ACT – Australia)
Eight Hours Day (TAS – Australia)
Start of Holi Festival (India, Nepal, Sri Lanka)

TUESDAY 14

WEDNESDAY 15

Revolution Day (Hungary)

THURSDAY 16

FRIDAY 17

St Patrick's Day

Plan an Adventure

SATURDAY 18

SUNDAY 19

Feast of St Joseph (Malta)

Like all great travellers, I have seen more than I remember, and remember more than I have seen. – Benjamin Disraeli

March 2017

MONDAY 20

March Equinox

TUESDAY 21

Human Rights' Day (South Africa)

WEDNESDAY 22

THURSDAY 23

FRIDAY 24

Plan an Adventure

SATURDAY 25

Independence Day (Cyprus, Greece)

SUNDAY 26

Mothering Sunday (Ireland, UK)
Start of Daylight Saving Time (Ireland, UK)

I never travel without my diary. One should always have something sensational to read in the train. – Oscar Wilde

Gokyo Lakes, NEPAL

The Gokyo Lakes within Sagarmatha National Park sit at the head of the Dudh Kosi Valley, and provide a spectacular trekking alternative to the popular Everest Base Camp route. Tranquil trails wind through the Sherpa heartland, and from Gokyo Ri's summit there are sublime views to the top of the world.

© Feng Wei Photography / Getty Images

Amboseli National Park, KENYA

Amboseli belongs in the elite of Kenya's national parks, and it's easy to see why. Its signature attraction is the sight of its countless big-tusked elephants and, if the weather permits, the dramatic backdrop of Kilimanjaro. You'll also see wildebeest and zebras, and perhaps even lions.

© Jonathan Gregson

March / April 2017

MONDAY 27

TUESDAY 28

WEDNESDAY 29

THURSDAY 30

FRIDAY 31

Freedom Day (Malta)

Plan an Adventure

SATURDAY 1

Greek Cypriot Day (Cyprus)

SUNDAY 2

End of Daylight Saving Time (Australia, New Zealand)

One way to get the most out of life is to look upon it as an adventure. – **William Feather**

April 2017

MONDAY 3

TUESDAY 4

WEDNESDAY 5

THURSDAY 6

FRIDAY 7

Plan an Adventure

SATURDAY 8

SUNDAY 9

All travel has its advantages. If the passenger visits better countries, he may learn to improve his own. And if fortune carries him to worse, he may learn to enjoy it. – Samuel Johnson

April 2017

MONDAY 10

TUESDAY 11

Start of Passover

WEDNESDAY 12

THURSDAY 13

Maundy Thursday
Songkran Water Festival (Thailand)

FRIDAY 14

Good Friday (except Ireland)

Plan an Adventure

SATURDAY 15

SUNDAY 16

Easter Sunday

*When you travel, remember that a foreign country is not designed to make you comfortable.
It is designed to make its own people comfortable.* – Clifton Fadiman

April 2017

MONDAY 17

Easter Monday (except Scotland)

TUESDAY 18

End of Passover

WEDNESDAY 19

THURSDAY 20

FRIDAY 21

Plan an Adventure

SATURDAY 22

SUNDAY 23

St George's Day (England)

Every exit is an entry somewhere else. – Tom Stoppard

April 2017

MONDAY 24

Isra and Mi'raj
Yom HaShoah

TUESDAY 25

ANZAC Day Holiday (Australia, New Zealand)
Liberation Day (Italy, Portugal)

WEDNESDAY 26

Start of New Orleans Jazz & Heritage Festival (LA – USA)

THURSDAY 27

Resistance Day (Slovenia)
Freedom Day (South Africa)
King's Birthday (Netherlands)

FRIDAY 28

Plan an Adventure

SATURDAY 29

SUNDAY 30

I dislike feeling at home when I am abroad. – George Bernard Shaw

May 2017

MONDAY 1

May Day

TUESDAY 2

WEDNESDAY 3

Constitution Day (Poland)

THURSDAY 4

Declaration of Independence Day (Latvia)

FRIDAY 5

Plan an Adventure

SATURDAY 6

St George's Day (Bulgaria)

SUNDAY 7

Not all those who wander are lost. – J.R.R. Tolkien

May 2017

MONDAY 8

Victory Day (France)
Liberation Day (Czech Republic, Slovakia)

TUESDAY 9

WEDNESDAY 10

THURSDAY 11

FRIDAY 12

Plan an Adventure

SATURDAY 13

SUNDAY 14

Mothers' Day (Australia, Canada, New Zealand, USA)

It is better to travel well than to arrive. – **Buddha**

Petra, JORDAN

The ancient Nabataean city of Petra, with its elaborate architecture chiselled out of the pink-hued cliffs, is not just the leading highlight of a country blessed with more than its fair share of top sites: it's a wonder of the world. It lay forgotten for centuries, known only to the Bedouin who made it their home, until the great Swiss explorer Jean Louis Burckhardt happened upon it in 1812.

© Mark Read

Istanbul, TURKEY

This magical meeting place of East and West has more top-drawer attractions than it has minarets (and that's a lot). The conquering armies of ancient times tended to ransack instead of endowing with treasures, but that changed with the Byzantines and Ottomans. The latter's magnificently decorated imperial mosques are architectural triumphs that form one of the world's great skylines.

© Matt Munro

May 2017

MONDAY 15

TUESDAY 16

WEDNESDAY 17

THURSDAY 18

FRIDAY 19

Plan an Adventure

SATURDAY 20

SUNDAY 21

All journeys have secret destinations of which the traveller is unaware. – Martin Buber

May 2017

MONDAY 22

Victoria Day (Canada)

TUESDAY 23

WEDNESDAY 24

Culture & Literacy Day (Bulgaria)

THURSDAY 25

FRIDAY 26

Plan an Adventure

SATURDAY 27

Start of Ramadan

SUNDAY 28

Travel brings power and love back into your life. – Rumi

May / June 2017

MONDAY 29

Memorial Day (USA)
Spring Bank Holiday (UK)

TUESDAY 30

WEDNESDAY 31

THURSDAY 1

FRIDAY 2

Plan an Adventure

SATURDAY 3

SUNDAY 4

We live in a wonderful world that is full of beauty, charm and adventure. There is no end to the adventures we can have if only we seek them with our eyes open. – Jawaharlal Nehru

June 2017

MONDAY 5

Constitution Day (Denmark)
Western Australia Day (WA – Australia)

TUESDAY 6

National Day (Sweden)

WEDNESDAY 7

Sette Giugno (Malta)

THURSDAY 8

Bonnaroo Music & Arts Festival (TN – USA)

FRIDAY 9

Plan an Adventure

SATURDAY 10

SUNDAY 11

A good traveller has no fixed plans and is not intent on arriving. – Lao Tzu

June 2017

MONDAY 12

Queen's Birthday (Australia, except QLD, WA)

TUESDAY 13

WEDNESDAY 14

THURSDAY 15

FRIDAY 16

Youth Day (South Africa)

Plan an Adventure

SATURDAY 17

SUNDAY 18

Fathers' Day (Canada, UK, USA)

There are no foreign lands. It is the traveller only who is foreign.
– Robert Louis Stevenson

June 2017

MONDAY 19

TUESDAY 20

WEDNESDAY 21

June Solstice
Start of Glastonbury Festival (England)

THURSDAY 22

FRIDAY 23

Victory Day (Estonia)
Midsummer's Eve (Latvia)
Grand Duke's Birthday (Luxembourg)

Plan an Adventure

SATURDAY 24

St John's Day (Estonia, Latvia, Lithuania)

SUNDAY 25

End of Ramadan
National Day (Slovenia)

A journey is like marriage. The certain way to be wrong is to think you control it. – John Steinbeck

June / July 2017

MONDAY 26

TUESDAY 27

WEDNESDAY 28

THURSDAY 29

Feast of St Peter and St Paul (Malta)

FRIDAY 30

Plan an Adventure

SATURDAY 1

Canada Day (Canada)

SUNDAY 2

It is not down in any map; true places never are. – Herman Melville

Noosa National Park, AUSTRALIA

Featuring a string of perfect bays fringed with sand and pandanus trees, surfers come here for the long, rolling waves. Lovely hiking trails also criss-cross the park: top is the coastal trail to Hell's Gates, where you might spy koalas in trees around Tea Tree Bay and dolphins swimming off the rocky headland.

© Matt Munro

Lóngjǐ, Guǎngxī, CHINA

This part of Guǎngxī is famous for its breathtaking vistas of terraced paddy fields cascading in swirls down into a valley. You'll find the most spectacular views around the villages of Píng'ān, a sprawling Zhuàng settlement, the more remote Dàzhài, a mesmerising Yáo village, and Tiántóuzhài, atop a mountain.

© Mark Read

July 2017

MONDAY 3

Start of The Championships (Wimbledon – England)

TUESDAY 4

Independence Day (USA)

WEDNESDAY 5

St Cyril and St Methodius' Day (Czech Republic, Slovakia)

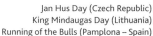

THURSDAY 6

Jan Hus Day (Czech Republic)
King Mindaugas Day (Lithuania)
Running of the Bulls (Pamplona – Spain)

FRIDAY 7

Plan an Adventure

SATURDAY 8

SUNDAY 9

We wander for distraction, but we travel for fulfilment. – Hilare Belloc

July 2017

MONDAY 10

TUESDAY 11

WEDNESDAY 12

Battle of the Boyne (Northern Ireland)

THURSDAY 13

FRIDAY 14

Bastille Day (France)

Plan an Adventure

SATURDAY 15

SUNDAY 16

People don't take trips…trips take people. – John Steinbeck

July 2017

MONDAY 17

TUESDAY 18

WEDNESDAY 19

THURSDAY 20

FRIDAY 21

National Day (Belgium)

Plan an Adventure

SATURDAY 22

SUNDAY 23

Bizarre travel plans are dancing lessons from God. – Kurt Vonnegut

July 2017

MONDAY 24

TUESDAY 25

WEDNESDAY 26

THURSDAY 27

Start of Tomorrowland Music Festival (Boom – Belgium)

FRIDAY 28

Start of Gilroy Garlic Festival (CA – USA)

Plan an Adventure

SATURDAY 29

SUNDAY 30

Certainly, travel is more than the seeing of sights; it is a change that goes on, deep and permanent, in the ideas of living. – Mary Ritter Beard

July / August 2017

MONDAY 31

TUESDAY 1

WEDNESDAY 2

THURSDAY 3

FRIDAY 4

Start of Edinburgh Festival (Scotland)

Plan an Adventure

SATURDAY 5

SUNDAY 6

The journey not the arrival matters. – T.S. Eliot

August 2017

MONDAY 7

Civic Holiday (Canada)
August Bank Holiday (Scotland)
Bank Holiday (ACT, NSW – Australia)
Picnic Holiday (NT – Australia)

TUESDAY 8

WEDNESDAY 9

Women's Day (South Africa)

THURSDAY 10

FRIDAY 11

Plan an Adventure

SATURDAY 12

SUNDAY 13

The world is a book and those who do not travel read only one page. – St Augustine

August 2017

MONDAY 14

TUESDAY 15

WEDNESDAY 16

THURSDAY 17

FRIDAY 18

Plan an Adventure

SATURDAY 19

SUNDAY 20

National Day (Hungary)
Independence Restoration Day (Estonia)

Wherever you go, go with all your heart. – Confucius

New York City, USA

Epicenter of art. Dining and shopping capital. Trendsetter. New York dons many crowns, and spreads an irresistible feast for all. When the sun sinks beyond the Hudson and luminous skyscrapers light up the night, NYC transforms into one grand stage. If you can dream it up, it's likely to be happening here.

© Matt Munro

Lofoten Islands, NORWAY

You'll never forget your first approach to the Lofoten Islands by ferry. The islands spread their tall, craggy physique against the sky like some spiky sea dragon and you wonder how human beings eke out a living in such seemingly inhospitable surroundings. The beauty of this place is simply staggering.

© Justin Foulkes

August 2017

MONDAY 21

TUESDAY 22

WEDNESDAY 23

THURSDAY 24

FRIDAY 25

Plan an Adventure

SATURDAY 26

SUNDAY 27

*I travel not to go anywhere, but to go. I travel for travel's sake.
The great affair is to move.* – Robert Louis Stevenson

August / September 2017

MONDAY 28

Start of Burning Man Festival (NV – USA)
August Bank Holiday (England, Wales, Northern Ireland)

TUESDAY 29

Slovak National Uprising Day (Slovakia)

WEDNESDAY 30

La Tomatina Festival (Spain)

THURSDAY 31

FRIDAY 1

Eid-al-Adha
Constitution Day (Slovakia)

Plan an Adventure

SATURDAY 2

SUNDAY 3

Fathers' Day (Australia, New Zealand)

It is good to have an end to journey toward; but it is the journey that matters, in the end. – Ernest Hemingway

September 2017

MONDAY 4

Labour Day (Canada, USA)

TUESDAY 5

WEDNESDAY 6

Unification Day (Bulgaria)
Cascamorras (Granada – Spain)

THURSDAY 7

FRIDAY 8

Feast of Our Lady of Victories (Malta)

Plan an Adventure

SATURDAY 9

SUNDAY 10

I have found out that there ain't no surer way to find out whether you like people or hate them than to travel with them. – Mark Twain

September 2017

MONDAY 11

Ethiopian New Year (2010)

TUESDAY 12

WEDNESDAY 13

THURSDAY 14

FRIDAY 15

Virgin Mary of the Seven Sorrows Day (Slovakia)

Plan an Adventure

SATURDAY 16

SUNDAY 17

Travel makes one modest, you see what a tiny place you occupy in the world.
– Gustave Flaubert

September 2017

MONDAY 18

TUESDAY 19

WEDNESDAY 20

THURSDAY 21

Al-Hijira
Rosh Hashanah
Independence Day (Malta)

FRIDAY 22

September Equinox
Independence Day (Bulgaria)

Plan an Adventure

SATURDAY 23

Oktoberfest (Munich – Germany)

SUNDAY 24

Heritage Day (South Africa)
Start of Daylight Saving Time (New Zealand)

Make voyages! Attempt them…there's nothing else. – **Tennessee Williams**

September / October 2017

MONDAY 25

Family & Community Day (ACT – Australia)

TUESDAY 26

WEDNESDAY 27

Meskel (Ethiopia)

THURSDAY 28

Czech Statehood Day (Czech Republic)

FRIDAY 29

Plan an Adventure

SATURDAY 30

Yom Kippur

SUNDAY 1

Ashura
Independence Day (Cyprus)
Start of Daylight Saving Time (Australia)

Travel is glamorous only in retrospect. – Paul Theroux

October 2017

MONDAY 2

Queen's Birthday (QLD, WA – Australia)
Labour Day (ACT, NSW, SA – Australia)

TUESDAY 3

Unity Day (Germany)

WEDNESDAY 4

Sukkot

THURSDAY 5

FRIDAY 6

Start of Austin City Limits Music Festival (TX – USA)

Plan an Adventure

SATURDAY 7

Alberquerque International Balloon Fiesta (NM – USA)

SUNDAY 8

Adventure is worthwhile in itself. – Amelia Earhart

Bay of Islands, NEW ZEALAND

Turquoise waters lapping, dolphins frolicking, pods of orcas gracefully gliding: these are the kinds of sights that the Bay of Islands delivers. Whether you're a hardened sea dog or a confirmed landlubber, there are myriad options to tempt you out onto the water to explore the gorgeous bay's 150-odd islands.

© Mark Read

Bagan, MYANMAR

More than 3000 Buddhist temples are scattered across the plains of Bagan, site of the first Burmese kingdom. Dating back to between the 11th and 13th centuries, many temples remain active religious sites and places of pilgrimage. Despite some modern renovations, Bagan continues to be a wonder.

© Andrew Montgomery

October 2017

MONDAY 9

Columbus Day (USA)
Thanksgiving Day (Canada)

TUESDAY 10

WEDNESDAY 11

THURSDAY 12

Hispanic Day (Spain)

FRIDAY 13

Plan an Adventure

SATURDAY 14

SUNDAY 15

For the born traveller, travelling is a besetting vice. Like other vices, it is imperious, demanding its victim's time, money, energy and the sacrifice of comfort. – Aldous Huxley

October 2017

MONDAY 16

TUESDAY 17

WEDNESDAY 18

THURSDAY 19

Diwali
FRIDAY 20

Plan an Adventure

SATURDAY 21

SUNDAY 22

*The real voyage of discovery consists not in seeking new landscapes,
but in having new eyes.* – Marcel Proust

October 2017

MONDAY 23

Republic Day (Hungary)
Labour Day (New Zealand)

TUESDAY 24

WEDNESDAY 25

THURSDAY 26

National Day (Austria)

FRIDAY 27

Plan an Adventure

SATURDAY 28

Ochi Day (Cyprus, Greece)
Independent Czechoslovak State Day (Czech Republic)

SUNDAY 29

End of Daylight Saving Time (Ireland, UK)

The first condition of understanding a foreign country is to smell it. – Rudyard Kipling

October / November 2017

MONDAY 30

TUESDAY 31

Halloween
Reformation Day (Slovenia)

WEDNESDAY 1

Day of the Dead (Mexico)

THURSDAY 2

FRIDAY 3

Plan an Adventure

SATURDAY 4

All Saints Day
Remembrance Day (Slovenia)

SUNDAY 5

Guy Fawkes Night (England)

A ship is safe in harbor, but that is not what ships are built for. – **William G.T. Shedd**

November 2017

MONDAY 6

TUESDAY 7

WEDNESDAY 8

THURSDAY 9

FRIDAY 10

Plan an Adventure

SATURDAY 11

Veterans' Day (USA)
Remembrance Day (Commonwealth)

SUNDAY 12

Remembrance Sunday (UK)

To awaken quite alone in a strange town is one of the pleasantest sensations in the world. – Freya Stark

November 2017

MONDAY 13

TUESDAY 14

WEDNESDAY 15

THURSDAY 16

FRIDAY 17

Freedom & Democracy Day (Czech Republic, Slovakia)

Plan an Adventure

SATURDAY 18

Proclamation of the Republic (Latvia)

SUNDAY 19

The use of traveling is to regulate imagination by reality, and instead of thinking how things may be, to see them as they are. – Samuel Johnson

November 2017

MONDAY 20

TUESDAY 21

WEDNESDAY 22

THURSDAY 23

Thanksgiving Day (USA)

FRIDAY 24

Plan an Adventure

SATURDAY 25

SUNDAY 26

Perhaps travel cannot prevent bigotry, but by demonstrating that all peoples cry, laugh, eat, worry, and die, it can introduce the idea that if we try and understand each other, we may even become friends. – Maya Angelou

Bavaria, GERMANY

From the cloud-shredding Alps to the fertile Danube plain, Bavaria is a place that keeps its clichéd promises. Story-book castles poke through dark forest, cowbells tinkle in flower-filled meadows, the thwack of palm on lederhosen accompanies the clump of frothy stein on timber benches, and medieval walled towns go about their time-warped business.

© Andrew Montgomery

November / December 2017

MONDAY 27

TUESDAY 28

WEDNESDAY 29

THURSDAY 30

St Andrew's Day (Scotland)

FRIDAY 1

National Day (Romania)
Independence Restoration Day (Portugal)

Plan an Adventure

SATURDAY 2

SUNDAY 3

We shall not cease from our exploring and the end of all our exploring will be to arrive where we started and know the place for the first time. – T.S. Eliot

December 2017

MONDAY 4

TUESDAY 5

WEDNESDAY 6

Constitution Day (Spain)
Independence Day (Finland)

THURSDAY 7

FRIDAY 8

Immaculate Conception

Plan an Adventure

SATURDAY 9

SUNDAY 10

Never go on trips with anyone you do not love. – Ernest Hemingway

December 2017

MONDAY 11

TUESDAY 12

Start of Hannukah

WEDNESDAY 13

Republic Day (Malta)

THURSDAY 14

FRIDAY 15

Plan an Adventure

SATURDAY 16

Reconciliation Day (South Africa)

SUNDAY 17

One of the great things about travel is that you find out how many good, kind people there are. – Edith Wharton

December 2017

MONDAY 18

TUESDAY 19

WEDNESDAY 20

THURSDAY 21

December Solstice

FRIDAY 22

Plan an Adventure

SATURDAY 23

SUNDAY 24

Christmas Eve

*I may not have gone where I intended to go, but I think I have
ended up where I intended to be.* – Douglas Adams

December 2017

MONDAY 25

Christmas Day

TUESDAY 26

Boxing Day
Day of Goodwill (South Africa)

WEDNESDAY 27

THURSDAY 28

FRIDAY 29

Plan an Adventure

SATURDAY 30

SUNDAY 31

New Year's Eve

Paris is always a good idea. – Audrey Heburn

World Time Zones

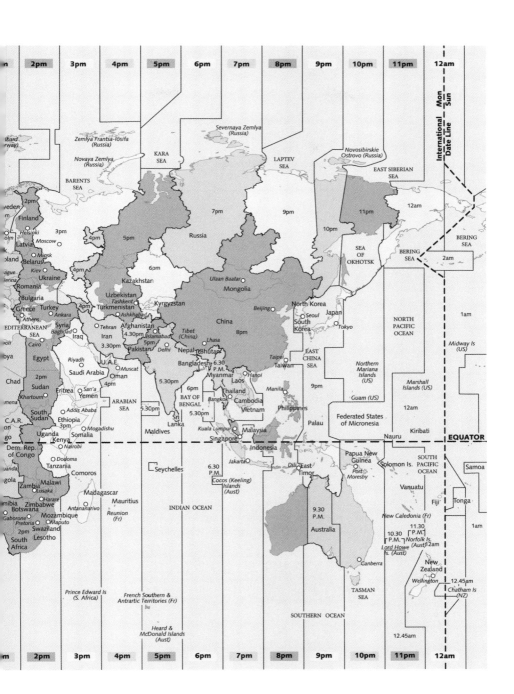

Published in July 2016 by Lonely Planet Publications Pty Ltd
ABN 36 005 607 983
www.lonelyplanet.com
ISBN 978 1 7603 4082 7
© Lonely Planet 2016
© Photographs as indicated 2016
Printed in China

Managing Director, Publishing Piers Pickard
Associate Publisher & Commissioning Editor Robin Barton
Design Lauren Egan
Layout Designers Campbell McKenzie, Mariana Sameiro
Editor Matt Phillips
Print Production Larissa Frost, Nigel Longuet

Thanks to Jessica Cole, Daniel di Paolo

All rights reserved. No part of this publication may be reproduced, stored in a retrieval system or transmitted in any form by any means, electronic, mechanical, photocopying, recording or otherwise except brief extracts for the purpose of review, without the written permission of the publisher. Lonely Planet and the Lonely Planet logo are trademarks of Lonely Planet and are registered in the US patent and Trademark Office and in other countries.

Lonely Planet offices
AUSTRALIA
Level 2 & 3, 551 Swanston St, Carlton 3053, Victoria, Australia
Phone 03 8379 8000 Email talk2us@lonelyplanet.com.au

USA
150 Linden St, Oakland, CA 94607
Phone 510 250 6400 Email info@lonelyplanet.com

UNITED KINGDOM
240 Blackfriars Rd, London SE1 8NW
Phone 020 3771 5100 Email go@lonelyplanet.co.uk

Although the authors and Lonely Planet have taken all reasonable care in preparing this book, we make no warranty about the accuracy or completeness of its content and, to the maximum extent permitted, disclaim all liability from its use.

Paper in this book is certified against the Forest Stewardship Council™ standards. FSC™ promotes environmentally responsible, socially beneficial and economically viable management of the world's forests.